She gave me love, as well as life;
so whatever goodness
I may bring to Earth
began with the gift
of my mother's heart.

— Robert Sexton

Blue Mountain Arts®
Other titles in this series...

Daughters

Friendship

Love

Sisters

Sons

A Blue Mountain Arts® Collection
to Let a Cherished Mother Know
How Much She Is Loved
and Appreciated

Edited by Patricia Wayant

Blue Mountain Press ™

Boulder, Colorado

Copyright © 2004 by Blue Mountain Arts, Inc.

All rights reserved. No part of this publication may be reproduced, stored in a retrieval system, or transmitted in any form or by any means, electronic, mechanical, photocopying, recording or otherwise, without the written permission of the publisher.

We wish to thank Susan Polis Schutz for permission to reprint the following poems that appear in this publication: "My Mother" and "You have shown me how to give of myself." Copyright © 1981, 1986 by Stephen Schutz and Susan Polis Schutz. All rights reserved.

Library of Congress Control Number: 2003116184
ISBN: 0-88396-835-5

Certain trademarks are used under license.
BLUE MOUNTAIN PRESS is registered in U.S. Patent and Trademark Office.

Manufactured in Thailand.
First Printing: 2004

 This book is printed on recycled paper.

Blue Mountain Arts, Inc.

P.O. Box 4549, Boulder, Colorado 80306

Contents

(Authors listed in order of first appearance)

There Is Nothing More Special than a Mother's Love

A mother's love is the treasury of our childhood; the star that guides our future; the gift of life itself.

Lincoln Andrews McArthur

*T*he love of a mother will see you through every heartache and worry. It will soothe, kiss, and hug away fears and sadness. It's a love that never disappears, even when everything else seems to ~ because the love of a mother is unconditional and never-ending.

Barbara Cage

Because of you, Mother,
I know the beauty of unconditional love.
Your love has always been
the most constant thing in my life.

From the time I was born,
you have always been there for me ~
    my source of warmth and comfort,
    my greatest encouragement,
    my biggest fan,
    my confidante,
    my best and truest friend...
        my precious mom.

You always had time for me...
    You still do.
You were always glad to see me
or hear from me...
    You still are.
You always believed in me...
    You still do.

For all that you are,
for all that you do,
for all your love,
I thank you with all my heart.

➢ Helen Vincent

No language can express
the power and beauty
of a mother's love.

Edwin Hubble Chapin

$\mathcal{M}$y mother's love is the kind that every child should grow up with. It never pre-judged me. It guided her to make decisions that always turned out to be fair, even if they didn't seem that way to me at the time.

My mother's love has believed in me, helped me, and accompanied me along the paths I've chosen since the day I first came into the world. Is there any way to repay her for all her years of love and caring, given so unselfishly?

My mother's love is in my heart every moment of my life. It means more to me than I'll ever be able to say.

— Jon Peyton

A mother's love has all the stars of heaven shining down on it at night.

Catherine Beecher

I don't recall the first time she held me
or when I first heard her voice.
But from the first moment
she held me in her arms,
she made the most selfless choice.

She chose to change her busy life
so that my life could begin.
She was my shelter from the rain;
on her, I could depend.

She held my hand when I was afraid
and helped me to mend my first broken heart.
She bandaged my wounds, wiped my tears,
and kept me from falling apart.

She loved me without question,
no matter what I did.
She shaped me into a confident adult
from such an awkward kid.

Even though she's not always right beside me,
her love is matched by no other.
And I am so thankful every day
that I have her for my mother.

— Stacey Swayze

What Is a Mother?

A mother is the illuminary that shines and weaves into the life of her children thoughts and feelings ~ rich, beautiful, grand, and noble.

Author Unknown

Mothers are...

Teachers, dreamers,
hopers, believers, coaches,
leaders, finders, seekers,
growers, bakers, movers, shakers,
followers, seers and keepers,
encouragers, helpers and speakers,
storytellers, excellent spellers,
amazing women,
and friends.

— Ashley Rice

*S*he is the guardian angel of the family, the queen, the tender hand of love. A mother is the best friend anyone ever has. A mother is love.

Author Unknown

$\mathcal{A}$ mother is someone who loves without condition and never gives up hope. A mother offers all she can give and expects nothing in return.

A mother works so hard and does so much. A mother never gives up no matter how big the struggle. A mother has laughter that can cheer up the world and a smile that can brighten a room. A mother can mend a broken heart and chase the clouds away.

A mother is loved more than words can express and appreciated each and every day by the people lucky enough to know her. A mother is a role model, an advisor, and a friend.

Elle Mastro

$\mathcal{A}$ mother is the truest friend we have when trials, heavy and sudden, fall upon us; when adversity takes the place of prosperity; when friends who rejoice with us in our sunshine desert us when trouble thickens around us.

Washington Irving

$\mathcal{M}$other, as I have grown, you have watched me experience all the joys and pains this world has to offer. You remained by my side every step of the way. You have always encouraged me, never doubted me, made me believe in myself, and never let me down.

You know me better than anyone else, and you're the first person I turn to when I need advice. You've listened to all my hopes and dreams: celebrating when they came true and comforting me when they shattered. You have taught me life's lessons and given me morals and standards to live by.

Your strength has helped me accomplish so much. You have handed me keys to open the doors of opportunity. When one door closes, I have the courage to open another, knowing that no matter what lies behind the door, I have your love, support, and friendship to turn to.

You have exceeded the duties of a mother and surpassed all expectations of a friend. You have been and always will be my best friend.

Sherrilyn Yvonne

A Mother Is Love Forever

A mother is someone amazing, wonderful, and wise. She is a source of so much pride and the center of family love.

A mother is guidance to listen to, reassurance to rely on, and joy to share.

A mother is a smile that stays inside you and a hand that is always holding your hand. A mother is someone who truly understands.

A mother is sweetness and strength. She is like a lighthouse, showing the way. She is like a harbor, enfolding you with a hug. Hers is the voice you want to hear when you're not sure what to do.

No one can chase the clouds away like a mother can. When you've made a mistake, no matter how big it's been, a mother's arms always open wide enough to take you in.

When you have happiness to shout about, news to talk about, plans to make, and dreams to dream, a mother is there to share every secret and care about every word.

A mother is a remarkable blending of beautiful thoughts and precious memories. She is the dearest of all people and the best of all friends.

A mother is a miracle that comes into your life the day you are born and that never ~ ever ~ ends.

Mothers are living proof that some things are priceless and some miracles really do come true.

~ Collin McCarty

Always There to Help and Understand

They might not need me;
  but they might.
I'll let my head be just in sight;
A smile as small as mine might be
Precisely their necessity.

Emily Dickinson

As I look back, I can see that when I was growing up it must not have been easy for my mother. But I could always count on her to be there for me: to support me, encourage me, and do everything in her power to give me anything I needed. She always put my needs ahead of her own.

Back then, I took it all for granted. I thought that was what all mothers did. Now I know how blessed I was to have a mother who loved me so much. Now I understand how hard she worked to give me all that she could and how much she sacrificed for me. Her unselfish giving showed me what love really means.

I want her to know that all she gave and all she did are deeply appreciated. I want to thank her for making a beautiful difference in my life.

Jason Blume

I always knew she would be there for me and that her love never depended on what I did or didn't do. She encouraged me to work toward my goals, and she helped me to have faith in my abilities. She made my growing-up years a very special time.

M. Joye

For as long as I can remember
she has been by my side
to give me support
to give me confidence
to give me help

For as long as I can remember
she has always been the person I looked up to
so strong
so sensitive
so pretty

For as long as I can remember
and still today
she is everything a mother should be

For as long as I can remember
she has always provided stability
    within our family
full of laughter
full of tears
full of love

So much of what I have become
is because of you, my mother
and I want you to know
that I appreciate you, thank you
and love you
more than words can express

                        Susan Polis Schutz

Mother, You Are the Strongest Person I Know...

I admire you ~ I admire your strength, your courage, your never-ending hope, and the way you never allow the clouds to block our sunshine. You have always been the light at the end of the tunnel, my constant support and source of love.

Even when the obstacles in our way seemed bigger than both of us, and I couldn't help but wonder if we'd make it through, you never stopped believing. You never quit. How can I ever thank you for that? How can I thank you for all the sacrifices you have made throughout my life?

Your dedication and commitment to making life better for us is truly admirable. In the hard times you get stronger. In the sad times you find a way to smile... and to make me smile, too.

You are one of the strongest women I know, and I only hope that I am just like you someday.

— Elle Mastro

Mothers Guide Us and Teach Us

My education was wholly centered in the glance, more or less serene, and the smile, more or less open, of my mother.

Alphonse de Lamartine

When I was young, my mother told me... "Look both ways before you cross the street ➳ Brush your teeth ➳ Be nice ➳ Be careful ➳ Just try your best ➳ Clean up your mess ➳ Go to sleep; it's after your bedtime ➳ Sleep tight ➳ Good night ➳ Sweet dreams ➳ I love you!"

But more importantly, she showed me what it's like to love someone and to be loved; how to give with all my heart and appreciate those who give theirs.

She taught me courage, to work hard, and if I only tried, I could do anything. She taught me forgiveness and gave me hope.

She inspired me and showed me all I deserved but also taught me humility. She showed me compassion, and from that I learned empathy.

She's given me so much and gotten so little in return. She is everything I could hope to be.

Brandi-Ann Tanaka

My first desire for knowledge and earliest passion for reading were awakened by my mother.

Charles Dickens

$\mathcal{M}$other, you could have just told me how to be and what to become, but instead you showed me how to question and choose my own destiny.

You could have left me alone when I was learning to walk, but you held my hands and shared in my joy, because it was your joy as well.

You read me stories and enjoyed my make~believe world, watching my creativity grow instead of closing that part of my mind.

You presented me with choices when I was wrong, and you gave me wisdom when I was mistaken.

You always let me try things my way, and in the times when I failed, you helped me to pick up the pieces and put them together another way.

You taught me how to turn failure into success.

You listened to all of my stories, and your patience taught me how to listen to others and really hear them.

You are a part of my every happiness and every tear.

There are no words to describe how much I will always love you.

Katie Bindschadler

It was she who planted and nurtured the first seeds of good within me. She opened my heart to the impressions of nature; she awakened my understanding and extended my horizon, and her percepts exerted an everlasting influence upon the course of my life.

Immanuel Kant

Mother, if you hadn't let me know when I did things that were wrong... If you had allowed me to make decisions that I wasn't old enough to make on my own... If you never opened your ears and listened when I had something to say... If I never had a mother like you, who cared enough to set me straight when I needed it... I wouldn't be the person I am today.

Because of you, and the firm but tender way you have loved me, I've been able to stand on my own and face the world with courage, strength, and self-assurance. I appreciate everything you've done for me... the lessons you've taught me and the consequences you made me pay when I broke the rules.

Throughout my life, you've been someone I've looked up to, believed in, and respected. More than anything, I thought it was important to tell you how much you've influenced me by leading me in a positive direction. If it weren't for you, I don't know where I would be today.

➤ T. L. Nash

How Do You Say Thank You to Someone So Special?

How do you thank someone who has given you the moon and the stars? How do you explain the deepest feelings of the heart? What do you say when the words don't even begin to convey the gratitude? With so much to express, where do you start?

Laurel Atherton

If I had a sky full of stars,
I'd give them all to you, Mother,
for all the times
you've blessed my heart.
If I had a garden full of flowers,
I'd tie them all with ribbons
and give them to you
just to celebrate your smile.
If I could, I'd plant a seed of love
and watch the happiness grow ~
just to show the world
how special you are.

Thanks for all the ways
you brighten my world
and always make me feel
so welcome and loved.
Thanks for all the ways
you make my heart feel
right at home
anywhere we are.
Thanks for all the ways
you are an angel to me.

Linda E. Knight

There are women who make things better simply by showing up. There are women who make things happen. There are women who make their way. There are women who make a difference. And women who make us smile. There are women who do not make excuses... women who cannot be replaced. There are women of wit and wisdom who, with strength and courage, make it through. There are women who change the world every day... women like my mother.

Ashley Rice

You worked so hard for our family. You loved us and sacrificed for us. I remember when your heart was broken at times. I wish I could have helped you more. If I could relive that part of my life, I'd show you better how much I loved you and appreciated you then. I would undo the things I did that were inconsiderate or unfeeling. I'd hug you more, thank you more, ask you more questions, and listen better.

If I ever took you for granted, I didn't mean to. Maybe I didn't know how to show love then, but now that I'm older, I hope you can see how much I love you and that I appreciate you more and more every day.

— Donna Fargo

Thank You, Mother, for My Beautiful Life

On the day I was born,
though I did not know it yet,
I was the one being blessed...

You are the one who helped me grow,
who picked me up when I fell.
You allowed me the freedom
    to experience for myself
what is right and wrong.

You guided me and protected me.
You showed me that a woman
    can be strong,
that she can be her own individual self,
and that she alone holds her destiny.

Your kind words were always so familiar.
You praised me when I succeeded
and encouraged me to continue
    striving for my goals
even though they sometimes seemed
    so out of reach.

You were always there.
You gave me a wonderful childhood.
Never once did you put yourself first.
You did more than expected,
and I thank you.

You are perfect in my eyes.
I adore you and admire you,
and I am proud to call you my mother.
Thank you for my beautiful life.

Joli Senical

I Love You, Mother

The years hold precious memories, but most of all, they hold growth. In a way, we grew up together. There's still some growing left to do, but one thing becomes clear to me with each passing day, and I hope you know: There's no other mother like you, and I love you very much.

Susan M. Pavlis

You have shown me how to give of myself
You have shown me leadership
You have taught me to be strong
You have taught me the importance of the family
You have demonstrated unconditional love
You have demonstrated a sensitivity
    to people's needs
You have handed down to me the important
    values in life
You have handed down to me the idea of
    achieving one's goals
You have set an example, throughout your life
of what a mother and woman should be like
I am so proud of you
and I love you
forever

                                    — Susan Polis Schutz

In more ways than I'll ever be able to say, I love you. All your life, you have been my guiding light: raising me and caring for me. You were there, like the angel that you are, holding all the ladders that reached to my stars and catching me every time I fell... If it weren't for you, I'm not sure I would know what love really is.

Laurel Atherton

$\mathcal{M}$other, within the shelter of your arms, I have found reassurance and encouragement and a precious kind of love. In the sound of your voice, I have heard guidance, understanding, and so much hope.

Every time I think of the smiles in your eyes, I am reminded of a happiness that is very essential to the family ties we share. In the bond that always lives on in our hearts, I have come to know how much I've always counted on you.

You brought me into the world and did everything you could to make it my very own heaven on earth. You have always done your very best to give me a feeling of self~worth and inner beauty. Even in the times when I may have caused you concern, you never gave up on me. I always felt you there; I always knew I was in your prayers and in your heart's warmest wishes.

To this very day, there is no one who gives such a sweetness to everything; no one anywhere who gives so much and asks so little in return; no one so much like an angel should be... than the mother... you are to me.

 Ceal Carson

For all the happiness you bring to my life, I wish the same and more for you. I can never come close to giving you as much as you've given me, but you always have my friendship and love.

Linda Sackett-Morrison

You give so much and love so completely. You have totally dedicated your life to being a good mother. I know there are things you didn't do for yourself that you'd like to have done and less-than-happy circumstances that you had to face. I'm sorry for every tear you cried and every disappointment you experienced. I'm sure I wasn't always as understanding as I should have been, and I apologize for not being more sensitive to you and your needs.

As I look back on my past, I see the many ways you helped me and all the things I learned from you. When I think about all those growing pains that I was going through, I see the most devoted mother in the world, and I have a renewed appreciation for you. I wouldn't be the person I am without your influence.

Thank you for giving me life. I am blessed to have been born to you, and I am thankful that you're my mother. I hope you never have a doubt about how much you mean to me. I love you with all my heart.

➤ Donna Fargo

I've always felt the light of her love
    shining on my days.
She's the brightest star in my sky ~
and her love will forever light my path
    and always guide my way.

Edmund O'Neill

No one compares with you, *Mother,*
when it comes to
being kind and giving
and helping to make
every day in the life
I am living... brighter, better,
and more of everything life can be.

I know I'll never be able
to truly thank you
for all the years of loving grace
you have blessed me with,
and for the gifts of keeping me
in your heart and for making
my happiness so complete.

I don't think I'll ever be able
to express all the feelings
inside me that wish
they could thank you
for the warmth you bring
and the smiles you inspire.

But I can let you know
that there isn't a mother
in all the world
who is loved more than you.

Anna Tafoya

ACKNOWLEDGMENTS

We gratefully acknowledge the permission granted by the following authors and authors' representatives to reprint poems or excerpts from their publications.

Robert Sexton for "She gave me love, as well as life...." Copyright © 1995 by Robert Sexton. All rights reserved.

Jason Blume for "As I look back, I can see that...." Copyright © 2004 by Jason Blume. All rights reserved.

Brandi-Ann Tanaka for "When I was young, my mother told me...." Copyright © 2004 by Brandi-Ann Tanaka. All rights reserved.

PrimaDonna Entertainment Corp. for "You worked so hard for our family" and "Mother, I Love You So Much" by Donna Fargo. Copyright © 2004 by PrimaDonna Entertainment Corp. All rights reserved.

A careful effort has been made to trace the ownership of selections used in this anthology in order to obtain permission to reprint copyrighted material and give proper credit to the copyright owners. If any error or omission has occurred, it is completely inadvertent, and we would like to make corrections in future editions provided that written notification is made to the publisher:

BLUE MOUNTAIN ARTS, Inc. P.O. Box 4549, Boulder, Colorado 80306.